HAND CONDITIONS AND EXAMINATIONS:

A RHEUMATOLOGIC AND ORTHOPAEDIC APPROACH

PROFESSOR DR MOHD SHAHRIR MOHAMED SAID
ASSOCIATE PROFESSOR DR SYAHRUL SAZLIYANA SHAHARIR
ASSOCIATE PROFESSOR DR JAMARI SAPUAN
ASSOCIATE PROFESSOR DR SHALIMAR ABDULLAH

PARTRIDGE

Library of Congress Control Number:		2021919471
ISBN:	Hardcover	978-1-4828-7918-6
	Softcover	978-1-4828-7919-3
	eBook	978-1-4828-7917-9

To order additional copies of this book, contact
Toll Free +65 3165 7531 (Singapore)
Toll Free +60 3 3099 4412 (Malaysia)
orders.singapore@partridgepublishing.com

www.partridgepublishing.com/singapore

PREFACE

This book is an interesting reading companion that explores the hand and wrist aspects of rheumatology and orthopaedics. Together with information from detailed articles and textbooks, this book can assist junior medical undergraduate students, postgraduate students, general practitioners, general physicians, and orthopaedic surgeons in the recognition of hand and wrist pathologies and treatment.

We hope that you enjoy the book as well.

ABSTRACT

This book is the brainchild of interdisciplinary collaboration between experts in the field of rheumatology and orthopaedics. The multifunctional hand plays such an important role in day-to-day life, to an extent where a slight deviation from its normal function may lead to disability. Understanding hand anatomy is essential to identify the causes of its dysfunction. Thus, we start by introducing the basic anatomy of the hand by recognising its bones and various important tendons of the fingers. The sections of this book then expand its coverage of rheumatology by enlightening readers with the mechanics and pathophysiology of deformities associated with rheumatoid arthritis, psoriatic arthritis, scleroderma, gouty arthritis, and osteoarthritis.

The orthopaedic section compliments this book with the various interventional modalities of hand and wrist pathologies. A true highlight of this book is a fully illustrated section on detailed physical examination of the hand. The concise examination techniques featured here will come in handy during patient consultations and also assist exam candidates to prepare for their short case stations. This section also includes real case images of classical clinical features and varied manifestations of respective hand and wrist disorders which are commonly encountered in medical practice. These high-quality images provide long-lasting visual memory of subtle diagnostic cues and at the same time help improve one's ability to make a bedside diagnosis. We have also included various images of orthopaedic surgical procedures which can be an excellent supplement to clinical case-based teaching.

Finally, we take a look into the role of radiology in the diagnosis of hand and wrist disorders and learn to recognise the common abnormalities which appear on the radiograph and ultrasound of the hand and wrist. All in all, this book is ideal for medical students in rheumatology or orthopaedics rotation and medical practitioners as it consolidates all information relating to hand and wrist pathology in one title.

CONTENTS

1.0

INTRODUCTION

Hand examination is a common short case in examination both in internal medicine and orthopaedics. Furthermore, it is often included as a station in undergraduate, Membership of Royal College Physician (MRCP), masters of internal medicine (MMed internal medicine), and also masters in orthopaedics.

In rheumatology, hand examination is different from GALS screening examination, as the examination focuses on diagnosing a disease from the hands and detecting disease complications.[1] To date, there are limited well-recognised or standardised methods of hand examination in medical examinations. Most often, an examination of the hands involves a running commentary style of presentation. Therefore, this manual is written to assist undergraduate and postgraduate students alike on how to approach hand examination in their respective examinations.

2.0

THE HAND

The human hand is made up of the wrist, palm, and fingers. Internally, the hand consists of twenty-seven bones, twenty-seven joints, thirty-four muscles, over one hundred ligaments and tendons, and many blood vessels and nerves.[2]

3.0

COMMON HAND CONDITIONS IN RHEUMATOLOGY

The prominent hand diseases in rheumatology are rheumatoid arthritis (RA), psoriatic arthritis (PsA), osteoarthritis (OA), systemic lupus erythematosus (SLE), systemic sclerosis (SSc), seronegative arthritis, and chronic tophaceous gout.

These arthritides can cause severe dysfunction and occasional deformities of the hands. Most often, these conditions can involve the joints as well.

Except for osteoarthritis, the above arthritides can occur before the age of forty and have the predilection to occur in one gender compared to the other. For example, except for chronic tophaceous gout, the other arthritides tend to occur more commonly in females than in males.[3]

The Heberden's and Bouchard's nodes, which are osteophytes, are typically found in hand osteoarthritis. Swan neck, boutonniere, Z deformities, and ulnar deviations are associated with RA and PsA, whereas sclerodactyly, as the name suggests, is associated with SSc.[4]

However, these diseases are systemic in their effects to the human body. The effect on the hand is just the tip of the iceberg.

4.0

PATHOPHYSIOLOGY OF RHEUMATOID ARTHRITIS DEFORMITIES

4.1. Proximal Interphalangeal and Distal Interphalangeal Joints in RA

4.1.1. Boutonniere Deformity

The name of this condition is derived from the description of the head of proximal phalanx protruding through a gap, alike a finger protruding through a buttonhole. RA damages all structures with synovial covering, which includes the joints, ligaments, cartilage, and tendons. The central slip of the extensor digitorum communis tendon is thus interrupted. This results in the separation of the lateral slips, and the head of the proximal phalanx pops through this gap. The lateral slips, which are also reinforced by the lumbrical and interosseous muscles, volarly slide to the axis of the proximal interphalangeal (PIP) joint. The PIP joint will undergo forced flexion and an extension lag. This will be worsened by all the tendons that have traversed the PIP joint.[5]

The DIP, on the other hand, will undergo an extension lag soon after the disruption of the central tendon. The conjoint tendons of the DIP joints will then contract and cause a pathologic extension of the joint. The oblique retinacular ligament, which is located at the DIP joint, will eventually contract, contributing to hyperextensive changes of this joint.[6]

4.1.2. Swan-Neck (SN) Deformity

There are at least two classifications of SN deformities.

According to Nalebuff, there are four types:[7]
Type I—PIP joints are flexible in all positions.
Type II—PIP joint flexion is limited in certain positions.
Type III—PIP joint flexion is limited in all positions.
Type IV—PIP joints are stiff and have a poor radiographic appearance.

An alternative classification is by Welsh and Hastings, which states two types of the condition:[8]
Type I—caused primarily by PIP joint disease.
Type II—caused primarily by metacarpophalangeal (MCP) joint disease.

For this book, the Nalebuff classifications are used.

4.1.2.1. Nalebuff Type 1 Deformity

Patients with this type of deformity maintain the ability to flex the PIP joint because the origin of the deformity is at the PIP joint. This condition is caused by stretching of the capsule covering the flexor digitorum superficialis tendon due to synovitis or rupture of the tendon. As a result, restriction to the hyperextension of the mentioned joint is removed.[9]

However, if the synovitis process originates at the DIP joint, the stretching or rupture of the terminal extensor tendon to the distal phalanx gives rise to a mallet deformity. As a result, there is imbalance of the extensor tendon with relative over-pull of the central slip and laxity of the PIP joint's volar plate, resulting in hyperextension of the PIP joint.[10]

Treatments include conservative management using the Silver Ring or figure 8 thermoplastic splints. Alternatively, if these splints are not tolerated, the DIP joint can be fused with the PIP joint flexor tenodesis.[11]

4.1.2.2. Nalebuff Type II Deformity

In type II deformity, the PIP joint flexion is influenced by the position of the MCP joints. When the MCP joints are extended or radially deviated, passive PIP joint flexion is limited, but when flexed or ulnarly deviated, a greater degree of PIP flexion is possible. As RA progresses, radial deviation of the MCP and volar subluxation of the MCP joints occur, because of the increased tightness of the intrinsic muscles. As a result, a swan-neck deformity develops.[12]

The main principle of treatment is the relief of intrinsic tightness using surgical release.[13]

4.1.2.3. Nalebuff Type III Deformity

This type of deformity is characterised by significant reduction of PIP joint motion but with preserved joint spaces on radiographs. Stiffness is caused by the contracture of the extensor mechanism, the collateral ligaments, and the skin.

Treatment is PIP joint manipulation, lateral band mobilisation, and flexor tenosynovectomy or tenolysis.[14]

4.1.2.4. Nalebuff Type IV Deformity

Patients with this deformity have stiff PIP joints with radiographic advance intra-articular disease. Treatment require a salvage type of procedure, namely, arthrodesis or arthroplasty.[15]

4.2. Thumb Deformities (TD) in RA

Nalebuff and associates described six types of deformities of the thumb:[16]

Type 1 TD is a boutonniere deformity. It originates in the MCP joint and is associated with synovitis, dorsal hood disruption, and ulnarly subluxation of the extensor pollicis longus (EPL). The distal phalanx is extended as the proximal phalanx dorsally subluxes.[17] This is the most common TD in RA.

Type 2 TD is associated with hyperextension at the interphalangeal joint with subluxation of the carpometacarpophalangeal (CMC) joint.

Type 3 TD is a swan-neck deformity and is the second common type of TD in RA. The problem starts as a result of synovitis at the CMC joint, which causes the subluxation of the first MCP, both radially and dorsally. Thus, this joint will be adducted. When this adduction is combined with volar plate laxity, the MP joint hyperextends.

Type 4 TD is described as skier's thumb or gamekeeper's thumb, whereby synovitis of MP happens. This results in laxity of the ulnar collateral ligament, with or without adduction of the first metacarpal.

Type 5 deformity is similar to type 3 deformity, except that it does not involve adduction of the first metacarpal. It also starts in the MP joint and causes volar plate laxity, followed by MP hyperextension and IP joint flexion.

Type 6 deformity affects the IP joint and/or causes MP joint destruction with subluxation.

Treatment of TD depends on severity of the deformity and usually involves fusion rather than arthroplasty.[18]

4.3. The Metacarpophalangeal (MP) Joint in RA

The condylar structure of the MP joint permits motion in two planes. Therefore, they are unstable compared to the IP joints. The classic deformities are the ulnar drift and volar dislocation.[19]

Ulnar drift happens when the weakened radiocarpal ligaments cause radial rotation of the MP and carpus on its radius. This results in ulnar deviation of the MP joints via a unique mechanism termed as Z mechanism.[20] The Z mechanism describes the imbalance of opposing forces at a joint. Here, if a joint is angulated in one direction, the mirroring joint will adopt an opposite position if no physical barriers are present.[21] Subsequently, the extensor tendons can be dislocated in the ulnar direction and contribute to the ulnar drift.

Volar dislocation is caused by the weakening of the collateral ligaments and the dorsal extensor mechanism, when the extensor tendons are dislocated between the MP heads.

Conservative treatment is advised for RA of the MP joints as recurrence is always a possibility without proper control of the disease.[22] However, for early ulnar drift and volar dislocation, extensor tendon relocation with synovectomy is indicated.

4.4. RA of the Wrist

Significant synovitis of the wrist and the resulting destruction results in pain, reduced function, and deformities. RA of the wrist starts at the ulnar side, and synovitis destroys the ulnar carpal, stabilising ligaments. Furthermore, triangular fibrocartilage complex is attenuated, and the distal radial ulnar joint becomes eroded.[23] These result in caput ulna syndrome. This syndrome is described by dorsal subluxation of the distal ulna, volar subluxation of the extensor carpi ulnaris tendon, and supination of the proximal carpal bones.[24] Synovitis of the radial side produces attenuation of the radioscaphocapitate ligament with rotary subluxation of the scaphoid and ulnar translocation of the carpal bones. Thus, the hand deviates radially and stays in the supinated position, subsequently leading to the ulnar drift of the phalanges on the metacarpals.[25]

Treatment is synovectomy of the ulnar or radial carpal sites and, if necessary, a tendon transfer.[26]

4.5. Tenosynovitis in RA

The tendon sheath is covered in paratenon and synovium and often precedes the joint involvement in RA. Synovial proliferation results in fluid accumulation that eventually leads to thickening. This process weakens the tendon and leads to rupture.[27]

4.5.1. Flexor Tenosynovitis in the Fingers in RA

Synovial proliferation produces rheumatoid nodules on the tendons, resulting in trigger finger. There are four types of RA-related trigger finger (RATF). Type 1 is similar to non–RA stenosing tenosynovitis in which the tendons catch at the first annular pulley during flexion, because of the small localised hyperproliferation of the synovium. Type 2 is characterised by distal palmar nodules locking the finger in flexion. Type 3 happens when the flexor digitorum profundus nodules near the second annular pulley lock the fingers in extension. The final type is caused by generalised tenosynovitis within the fibro-osseous canal.[28] Treatments are flexor tenosynovectomy and nodule excision.

4.6. Tendon Ruptures in RA

The two main causes of tendon ruptures are chronic attrition of the tendon over bony prominence and synovial invasion of the tendon. The most frequent sites for extensor tendon rupture are at the distal end of the ulna and at the Lister tubercle.

4.6.1. Extensor Tendon Ruptures

Commonly affected extensor tendons are the extensor pollicis longus (EPL), extensor digiti quinti, and extensor digiti communis. Multiple ruptures of the extensor tendon begin frequently with the small finger extensor and proceed to extend radially. Hsueh et al. found in their retrospective study that the risk factors of tendon rupture includes RA that spanned over eight years in duration, continuous tenosynovitis lasting for more than one year, and a Larsen score of more than four.[29]

EPL tendon rupture is manifested by palpating the tendon at the wrist and asking the patient to extend the thumb with the palm resting on a flat surface. Deformity and functional loss warrant end-to-end repair, tendon graft, or tendon transfer.[30] However, there are three complications of hand RA that can mimic extensor tendon ruptures. Firstly, the MP joint dislocation; secondly, the volar and ulnar subluxation of the extensor tendons between the phalanges; and thirdly, paralysis due to posterior interosseous nerve compression. A reliable diagnostic differentiation test is the tenodesis effect, whereby extension of the MP joints occurs when the wrist is flexed.[31]

4.6.2. Flexor Tendon Ruptures in RA

The flexor pollicis longus is commonly affected in RA. Rheumatoid nodules can affect FDP by limiting its function, and this may cause rupture. Treatment is indicated if there is functional loss.[32]

Treatment of rheumatology hand condition will be a multidisciplinary approach involving the rheumatologists, orthopaedic surgeons, physiotherapists, and pharmacists.[33]

5.0

PSORIATIC ARTHRITIS (PSA) HAND DEFORMITIES

The deformities are similar to RA, but in PsA, the main pathophysiology involves the synovio-entheseal complex (SEC).[34]

6.0

HAND OSTEOARTHRITIS (HOA)

As an individual ages, tissues of the cartilage and bone disintegrate. The disintegrations compromise the structure and function of the joints and, combined with environmental factors such as mechanical loading or pressure on the joints, causes OA.[35] OA is classified into primary and secondary, termed as Heberden's and Bouchard's nodes, respectively. Heberden's nodes are the enlargement of the DIP joints, and Bouchard's nodes are the enlargement of the PIP joints.[36]

7.0

GOUTY ARTHRITIS HANDS (GAH)

Involvement of the hand in gouty arthritis (GA) is uncommon.[37] In GA, inflammation happens because of monosodium urate crystal deposition into the synovial, bursal, and cartilaginous tissue. As the inflammation progresses, erosions happen and destroy the joints. On the other hand, the tendon is usually entrapped or ruptured due to the presence of tophaceous deposits.[38]

8.0

SCLERODERMA HANDS (SH)

The hands of scleroderma patients have poor vascularised tissues and a reduced soft tissue envelope. Generally, they may have calcium deposits within the soft tissues that cause pain and may cause skin ulceration, digital ischaemia, digital gangrene, and joint contracture.[39]

Raynaud's phenomenon is closely associated with SH and is stimulated by cold or stress.

Moreover, calcinosis affects 22 per cent of scleroderma patients and is due to chronic inflammation or damage and underlying chronic ischaemia. The ischaemia is caused by vasospasm and irreversible micro- and macrovascular changes.[40]

9.0

OTHER COMMON HAND DISORDERS

9.1. Ganglion Cysts

Ganglion cysts are filled with gelatinous mucoid material and believed to have resulted from repetitive microtrauma.[41] These continuous microinjurious processes stimulate the formation of cysts from mesenchymal cells at the synovial capsular junction. Injury to the supporting capsular and ligamentous tissues stimulates fibroblasts to produce hyaluronic acid, which accumulates to further produce the mucin material.[42] They are the most common soft tissue mass found in the hands. Most often, these cysts are asymptomatic but may lead to pain, tenderness, weakness, or cosmetic issues. They occur three times more in women and are commonly found between the ages of twenty and fifty.

Seventy percent of ganglion cysts are found on the dorsal part of the wrist, arising from the scapholunate ligament or articulation. Interestingly, ganglion cysts can arise from the dorsal DIP joint and are associated with Heberden's nodules in osteoarthritis.[43]

Treatment is conservative for asymptomatic patients. For symptomatic patients, it is usually surgical dissection in an outpatient setting. Unfortunately, the recurrence rate is between 15 per cent and 20 per cent.[44]

9.2. Carpal Tunnel Syndrome (CTS)

According to Nigel et al., carpal tunnel syndrome is a myriad of symptoms and signs that arise following compression of the median nerve within the carpal tunnel.[45] Patients feel numb, paraesthesia, and pain in the median nerve distribution. Diagnostic investigations include electromyography, nerve conduction studies, ultrasound, and magnetic resonance imaging.[46]

The first kind of treatment consists of aerobic fitness and weight loss programme.[47] Mild to moderate stage of the disease can be treated with night-time wrist splinting for three weeks.[48] If this fails, then steroid injections into the carpal tunnel is indicated.[49] Finally, if everything else fails, surgical release of the transverse ligament is indicated and has shown to provide high initial success rates.[50]

9.3. Dupuytren's Contracture (DC)

This has always been the first step in all types of examination. From general inspection, many diseases and conditions can be diagnosed. According to Eva Kovacs et al., DC is caused by thickening and thus shortening of the palmar fascia, leading to digital contractures.[51] The site of DC is usually the ring and little fingers. This would mean that the patient will be unable to extend the fourth and fifth fingers. DC is commonly observed in people of Northern Europe descent,[52] aged more than fifty years,[53] bilateral (45 per cent), and if unilateral, the right hand is more commonly affected.[54] The ratio of males to females is 3:1, and this may be related to the expression of androgen receptors in the Dupuytren fascia.[55] Other potential risk factors include manual labour with vibration exposure, prior hand trauma, alcoholism, smoking, diabetes mellitus, hyperlipidemia, Peyronie's disease, and complex regional pain syndrome.[56] Rheumatoid arthritis is a negative factor for DC.

Phases of DC

1. Proliferative—pain is caused by proliferation of the myoblast and involves the nerve fibres or compression of local nerves.[57]

2. Involutional—the disease spreads along the fascia and into the fingers, resulting in the formation of a cord.[58]

3. Residual—the disease continues its spread and tightens the cord to create contractures.[59]

Severity of DC[60]

Grade 1—thickened nodule and band in the palmar aponeurosis.

Grade 2—development of pretendinous and digital cords.

Grade 3—presence of flexion contracture.

DC is treated with conservative medical and surgical modalities.[61]

10.0

EXAMINATION OF THE HANDS

10.1. General Inspection

In rheumatology, a careful general inspection can reveal systemic lupus erythematosus (SLE), scleroderma, and complications from prolonged steroid use, such as Cushing's syndrome. A candidate who is instructed to examine the hands should train himself or herself to have a good sense of general inspection.

The table below will assist the candidate in general inspection, prior to hand examination:

No.	Disease	Signs for Recognition
1	SLE	Malar rash, discoid lupus, Cushing's syndrome
2	Scleroderma	Tight and shiny facial skin, beaklike nose, microstomia, telangiectasia

3	Cushing's syndrome	Moon facies, acne

If key signs are recognised early, a disease can be diagnosed even before examining the hands. Stronger indications of a disease may then appear when the hands are examined. These ensures a smooth and professional examination.

10.2. Musculoskeletal Hand Anatomy[62]

10.2.1. The Bones

A detailed examination of the hand requires an essential knowledge of the anatomy of the hand.

The hand is comprised of twenty-seven bones, whereas the wrist is made up of eight carpal bones grouped in two rows. From radial to ulnar, the proximal row consists of the scaphoid, lunate, triquetrum, and pisiform bones. In the same direction, the distal row consists of the trapezium, trapezoid, capitate, and hamate bones. Mnemonically, they form the phrase 'She looks too pretty, try to catch her'. The scaphoid is the commonest bone to be fractured, and the lunate is the commonest bone to dislocate in the hand.

The hand also contains five metacarpal bones. Each metacarpal has a base, a shaft, a neck, and a head.

Distally, the hand contains fourteen phalanges. Each digit contains three phalanges (proximal, middle, and distal), except for the thumb, which only has two phalanges. Each digit is referred to by its name (thumb, index, long, ring, and small) rather than by number. This is to avoid confusion in the case a patient may have had a finger amputated. Moreover, some individuals prefer to refer the thumb as the first finger, whilst others, the index finger. It is also inappropriate to point to the finger involved during a clinical examination; thus, referring by each finger's name is more specific.

There may also be sesamoid bones present at the distal portion of the first and second metacarpals.

10.2.2. The Skin[63]

The dorsum of the hand has thin and pliable skin. Below this is a layer of areolar tissue where both the lymphatic and venous systems are located.

In contrast, the skin of the palmar surface is thick and hairless. It is attached to the underlying fascia by vertical fibres. Highly receptive sensory nerve organs are abundantly present here.

The skin is strongly attached to the deep structures at the palmar creases and is able to withstand shearing forces, allowing us to grip and hold items. Unlike the dorsal skin, which gets its blood supply from, the palmar skin gets its blood supply from vertical branches arising from the common digital vessels.

10.2.3. The Nails[64]

The nails are derived from the epidermidis. The components of the nail bed include the germinal matrix, sterile matrix, and hyponychium.

The germinal matrix produces the nail plate, which corresponds to the lunula. Externally, this is the pale semicircle in the proximal nail bed. This component extends from the proximal base of the distal phalanx to the insertion of the extensor tendon.

The sterile matrix is distal to the lunula, which is very vascular and produces 10 per cent of the nail plate's volume and strengthens the nails by producing squamous components.

The hyponychium, which is the distal part of the nail bed, adheres to the distal nail plate. This component has immune cells that resist infections to the nail plate.

The entire nail matrix is in close contact with the periosteum of the distal phalanx.

10.2.4. The Palmar Fascia and Deep Compartments

The palmar fascia has resistant fibrous tissue, which is arranged in longitudinal, transverse, oblique, and vertical fibres. These fibres arise from the palmaris longus tendon and extend to the base of each digit, where lesser amounts of fibres are attached to the tissues. These fibres and tissues form the fibrous flexor sheath and pulley system for each digit.

The transverse fibres are mainly found in the mid palm and web spaces. These fibres are associated with the longitudinal fibres that serve as pulleys for the flexor tendons, proximal to the digital pulleys.

The vertical fibres are attached to the palmar skin dermis. These fibres merge into septa, below the longitudinal and transverse fibres. They attach to the metacarpals, giving rise to eight different compartments for the flexor tendons and neurovascular bundles for each digit.

The Grayson and the Cleland ligaments are two fiscal bands located volar and dorsal to the neurovascular bundle of each digit, respectively. These fascial bands are located in a common central compartment, proximal in the palm.

10.2.5. The Nerves[65]

The hand is innervated by the median, ulnar, and radial nerves.

10.2.5.1. Median Nerve

The median nerve arises from C5 to T1 roots, forming the lateral and medial cords of the brachial plexus. In the hand, the median nerve is mainly responsible for thumb movements.

In the forearm, motor branches supply the pronator teres, flexor carpi radialis, palmaris longus, and flexor digitorum superficialis muscles. The anterior interosseus branch innervates the flexor pollicis longus, flexor digitorum profundus (index and long fingers), and pronator quadratus muscles. The anterior interosseous nerve (AIN) is purely a motor nerve. In AIN neuritis or AIN injury, the patient experiences pain in the forearm and is clinically unable to make out the OK sign due to the paralysis of the flexor pollicis longus and flexor digitorum profundus up to the index finger.

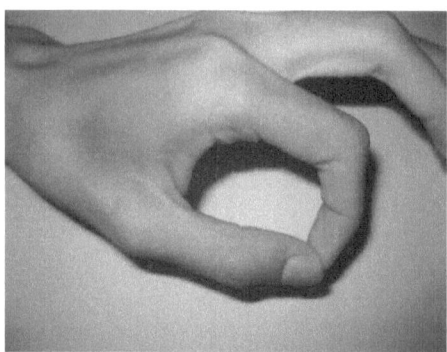

Figure 3. A patient demonstrating the OK sign.

Proximal to the wrist, the palmar cutaneous branch provides sensation at the thenar eminence. This nerve does not pass through the carpal tunnel; hence, in carpal tunnel syndrome, the sensation over the thenar eminence is intact. The recurrent motor branch supplies the thenar muscles (abductor pollicis brevis, opponens pollicis, and superficial head of flexor pollicis brevis) and the index and long fingers with lumbrical muscles. The sensory digital branches provide sensation to the thumb, index finger, long finger, and radial side of the ring finger. Some variations occur in the location of the recurrent motor branch of the median nerve. The motor branch mainly arises from the median nerve, distal to the distal part of the transverse carpal ligament. However, it may also arise under or pierce through the flexor retinaculum.

10.2.5.2. Ulnar Nerve[66]

The ulnar nerve arises from the C8 to the T1 roots, which form the medial cord of the brachial plexus. The ulnar nerve is mainly responsible for innervating the small muscles of the hand, allowing fine and precise movements.

The motor branches innervate the flexor carpi ulnaris and flexor digitorum profundus muscles to the ring and small fingers. Proximal to the wrist, the palmar cutaneous motor branch provides sensation to the hypothenar eminence.

At the distal forearm, the ulnar dorsal motor branch supplies sensation to the ulnar portion of the hand's dorsum, the entire small finger, and part of the ring finger.

In the hand, the digital nerves, which is a superficial branch of the ulnar nerve, innervates the small finger and ulnar of the ring finger. The deep motor branch passes through the Guyon canal together with the ulnar artery and supplies nerves to the hypothenar muscles (abductor digiti minimi, opponens digiti minimi, flexor digiti minimi, and palmaris brevis), all the interosseis, the two ulnar lumbricals, the adductor pollicis, and the deep head of the flexor pollicis brevis. The Guyon canal is an area where the ulnar nerve can be compressed.

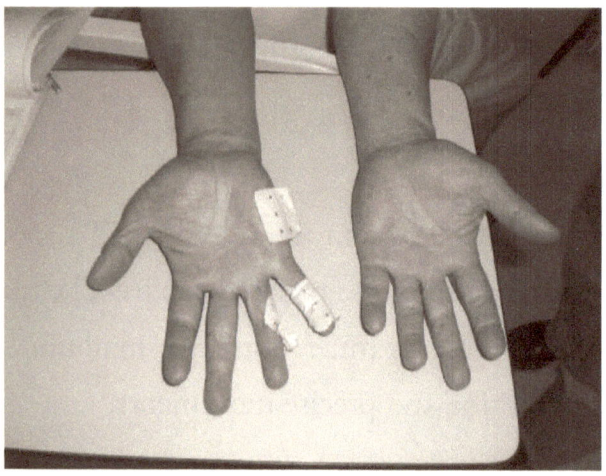

Figure 4. A patient with an ulnar nerve compression in the Guyon canal. Medicated plaster was applied over the ulnar nerve sensory distribution due to severe hypersensitivity, secondary to the compression.

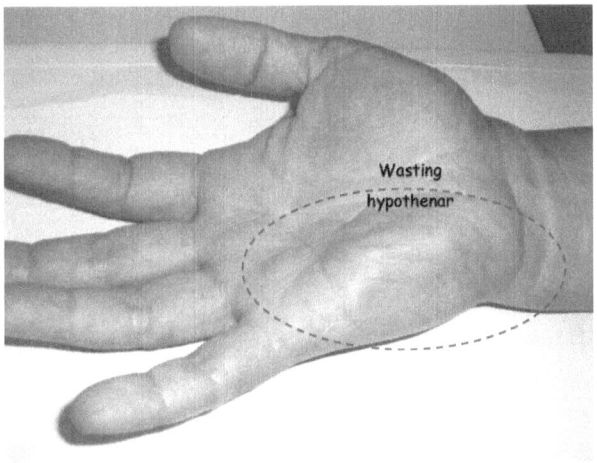

Figure 5. A patient with hypothenar muscle wasting
due to chronic ulnar nerve compression. Note
the dry skin over the ulnar nerve distribution.
This is due to the loss of autonomic control.

10.2.5.3. Radial Nerve[67]

The radial nerve is responsible for innervating the wrist,
finger, and thumb extensors.
It originates from C5 to T1 roots and form the posterior cord
of the brachial plexus (C6–8).

As the radial nerve travels into the axilla, it can be compressed,
producing a crutch or Saturday night palsy with weakness of
the triceps and wrist drop. Further distally at the mid-shaft
of the humerus, it is commonly injured in a spiral fracture of
the humerus.

At the elbow, the brachioradialis and extensor carpi radialis longus muscles are supplied with motor branches. At the proximal forearm, the radial nerve divides into the superficial branch of the radial nerve and posterior interosseous nerve (PIN).

The superficial motor branch provides sensation to the radial of the dorsum of the hand, the dorsum of the thumb, and the dorsum of the index finger, the long finger, and radial half of the ring finger proximal to the distal interphalangeal joints. The PIN supplies all the muscles in the extensor compartment: supinator, extensor carpi radialis brevis, extensor digitorum communis, extensor digiti minimi, extensor carpi ulnaris, extensor indicis proprius, extensor pollicis longus, extensor pollicis brevis, and abductor pollicis longus, except for the extensor carpi radialis longus, which is directly supplied by the radial nerve.

The PIN can be compressed at the opening of the extensor carpi radialis brevis, also known as the arcade of Frohse. Injury of the radial nerve will cause wrist and finger drop, whereas injury to the PIN will only cause finger drop. In radial nerve palsy, there is loss of sensation over the snuffbox. The radial nerve can be injured in the case of a fracture to the mid-shaft of the humerus.

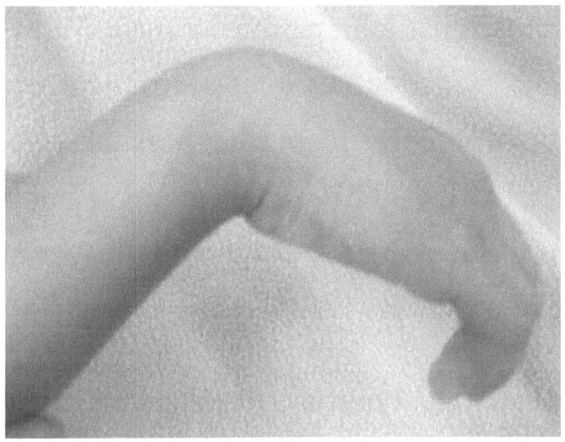

Figure 6. A patient with wrist drop,
secondary to radial nerve injury.

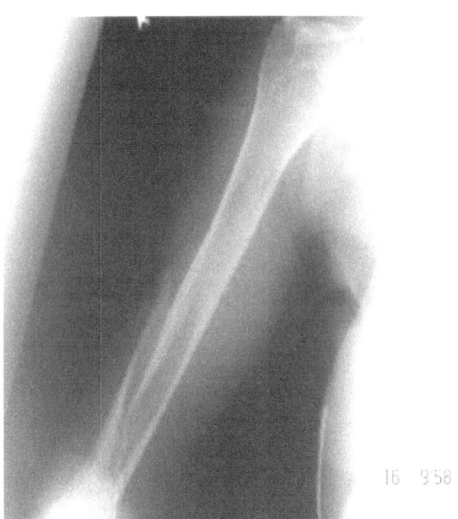

Figure 7. Radiograph of a spiral fracture of the
mid-shaft of the humerus, which is the most
common cause of radial nerve palsy.

10.2.6. Joints[68]

The distal radioulnar joint permits pronation and supination of the, as the radial bone rotates around the ulna. The radiocarpal joint consists of the proximal carpal bones and the distal radius. This former group of bones form the articulation surface with the radius and ulna, permitting the wide range of movements of the wrist joint.

The four distal carpal bones articulate with the metacarpals at the carpometacarpal joints. Only the first carpometacarpal joint is the most mobile. This joint is commonly involved in osteoarthritis, where patients are presented with pain at the base of the thumb when gripping items and mobilising the thumb.

Hyperextension is allowed by the volar plate, which attaches to the proximal phalanx.
At the interphalangeal joints, the volar plate limits extension.

10.3. Inspection of the Hands

Some diseases manifest as deformities of the hands, and some manifest as cutaneous signs of the hands.

No.	Disease	Hand Signs for Recognition
1	SLE	Swelling of the joints, vasculitic rash, and nerve involvement (median, ulnar, and radial)
2	Scleroderma	Tight and shiny skin, clubbing, pulp atrophy (nails longer than tip of finger), vasculitic rash, calcinosis
3	Rheumatoid arthritis	Swelling of the metacarpophalangeal and proximal joints, Z deformity of thumb, boutonniere and swan-neck deformities, ulnar deviation, and nerve involvement (median, ulnar, and radial)
4	Psoriatic arthritis	Can be similar as rheumatoid arthritis, has distal interphalangeal joint involvement, presence of dactylitis (sausage-like finger or toe), dystrophic nails, and psoriasis
5	Gouty arthritis	Swelling of the joints, presence of tophi near the joints.

| 6 | Dermatomyositis | Gottron papules and mechanic hands |
| 7 | Osteoarthritis | Bouchard's and Heberden's nodes at the proximal and distal interphalangeal joints of the fingers, subluxed first carpometacarpophalangeal (CMCJ) joint |

In the examinations, although candidates may be able to easily diagnose by inspection, they are still required to have differential diagnoses to support their provisional diagnoses.

Other observations include colour of the palms and the extensor region of the hands. This can help to determine whether the patient is pale or having palmar erythema.

Systemic Lupus Erythematosus Hands

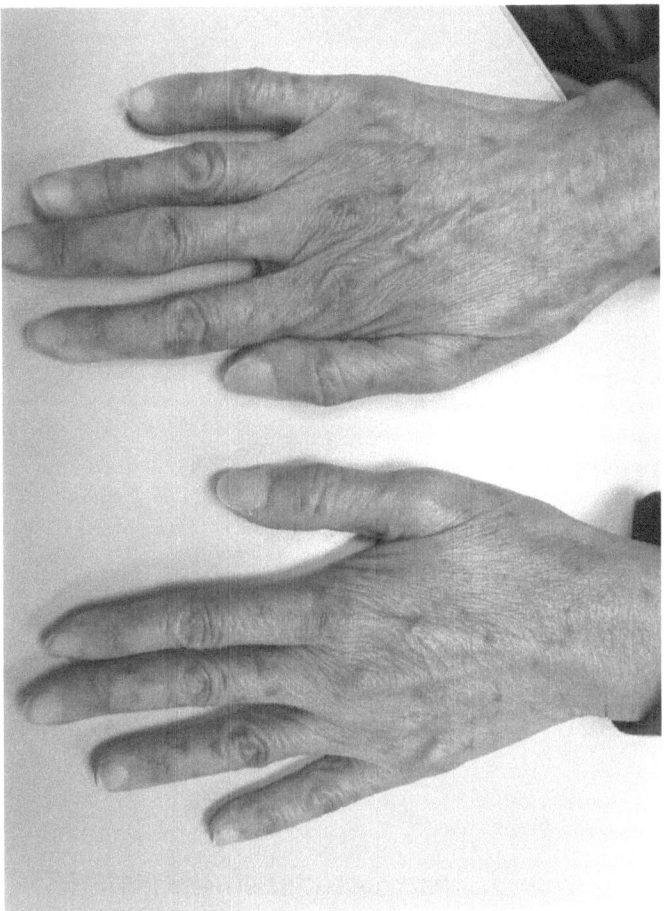

Figure 8. Systemic lupus erythematosus hands.

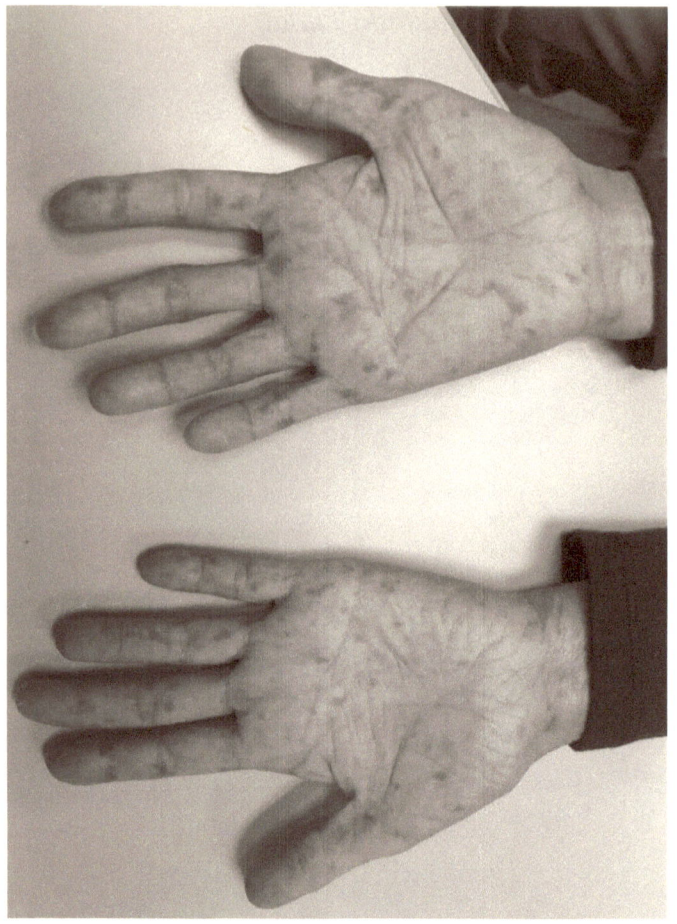

Figure 9. Systemic lupus erythematosus
hands with vasculitis.

Examination of the SLE hands mainly concentrates around describing abnormalities rather than full hand examination. However, neurology is essential because of vasculitic complications. The above pictures depict vasculitic lesions (Figures 8 and 9).

Scleroderma Hands

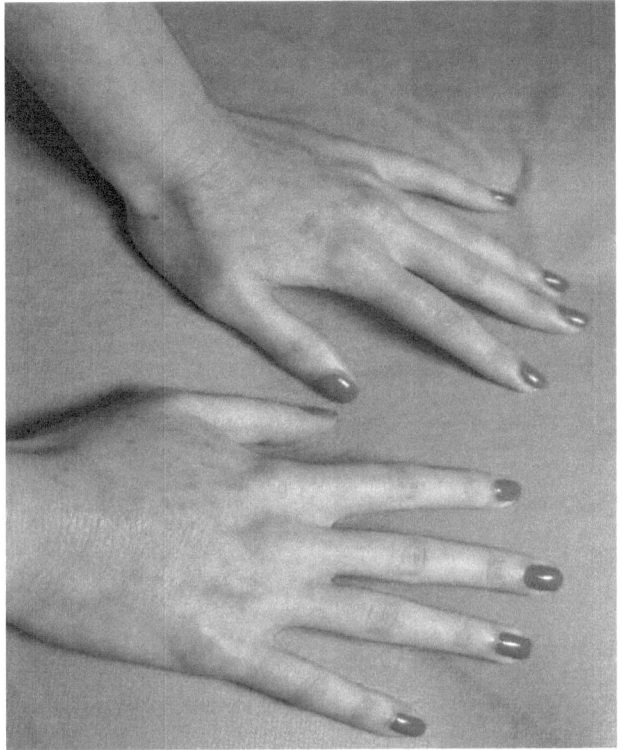

Figure 11. Sclerodactyly.

The above picture depicts sclerodactyly, namely, shiny and tight fingers. Scleroderma of the hands requires describing the abnormalities (e.g. sclerodactyly, pulp atrophy, vasculitis, and Raynaud's phenomenon). Neurology is important to rule out mononeuritis, which occurs secondary to vasculitis.

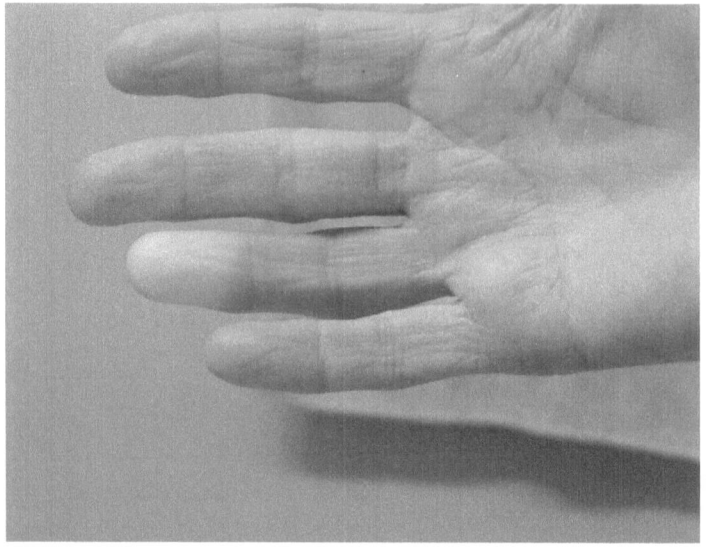

Figure 13. Raynaud's phenomenon.

The above picture is typical of Raynaud's phenomenon. However, in most instances, cold temperatures at the fingers are strongly suggestive of Raynaud's phenomenon.

Rheumatoid Arthritis Hands

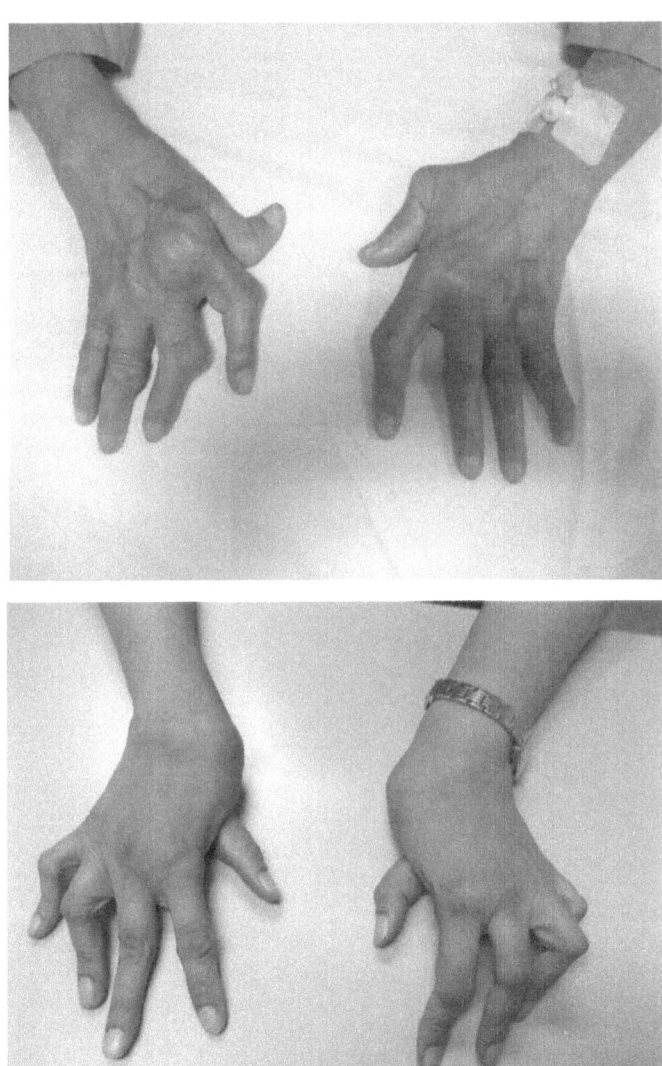

Figure 14. Rheumatoid arthritis hands.

The above picture depicts the classical findings of rheumatoid arthritis. In the examination of the hands, the presence of swan-neck, boutonniere, and Z deformities and metacarpophalangeal joint ulnar deviations are important signs to identify. The necessary steps consisting of inspections, neurology, tendon checks, and functional assessments are important in RA hand examinations.

Osteoarthritis Hands

This type of condition is infamous for Heberden's and Bouchard's nodes.

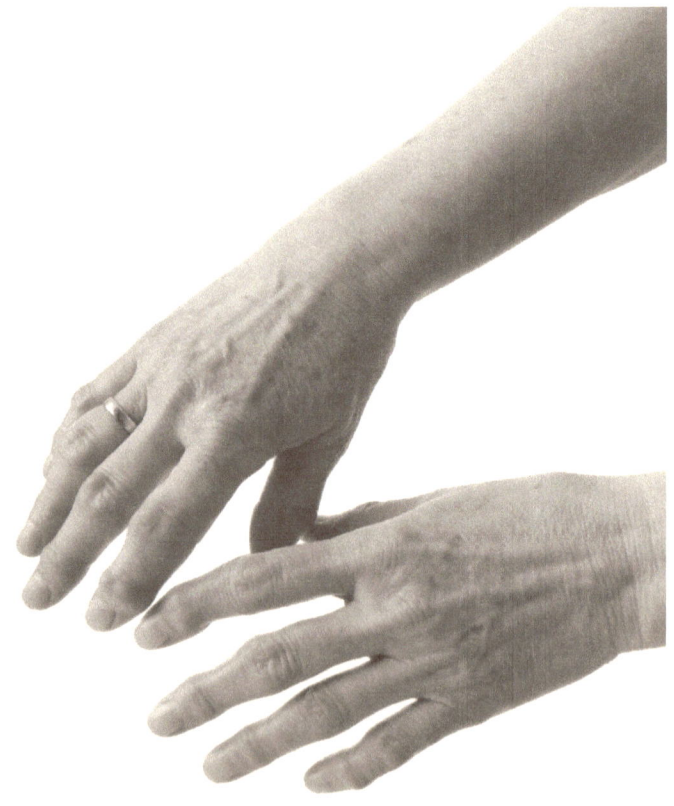

Figure 15. Osteoarthritis hands.

Dermatomyositis Hands

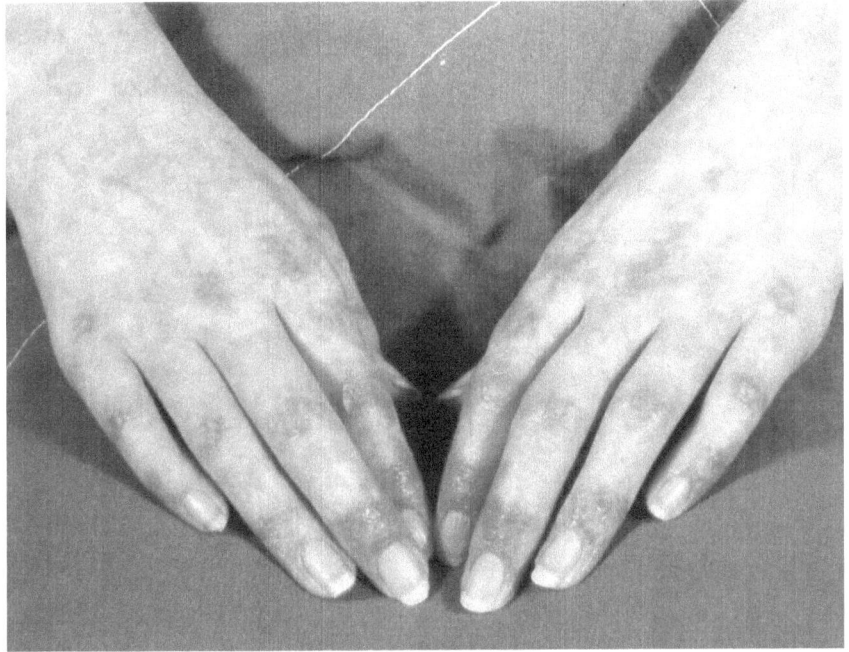

Figure 16. Gottron papules.

There is hyperpigmentation or erythematous lesions over the knuckle areas with Gottron papules in dermatomyositis hands. Neurology may be important.

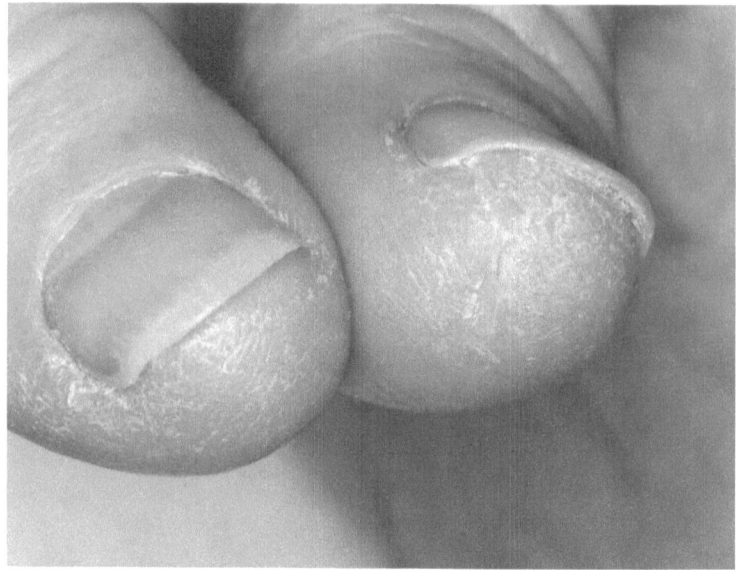

Figure 17. Mechanic's hands/fingers.

The above picture shows thickening, cracks, and fissures at the end of the fingers. Present here are also digital infarcts.

Psoriatic Arthritis

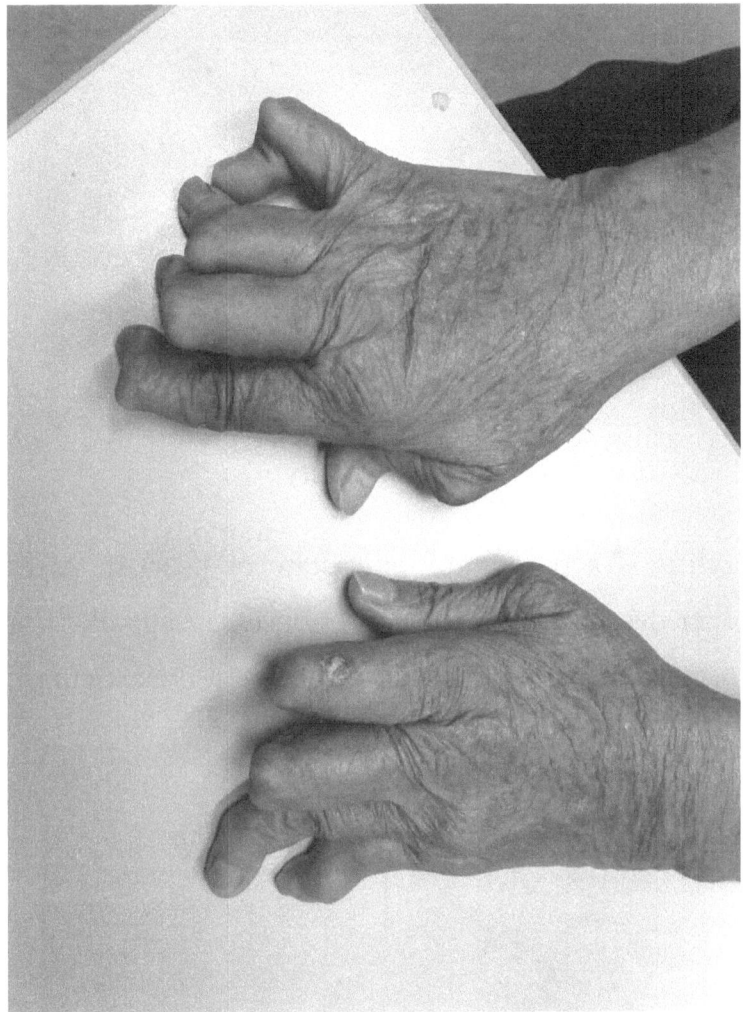

Figure 19. Arthritis mutilans.

The above pictures depict arthritis mutilans. All the steps of hand examination are essential to diagnose these typical types of psoriatic arthritis.

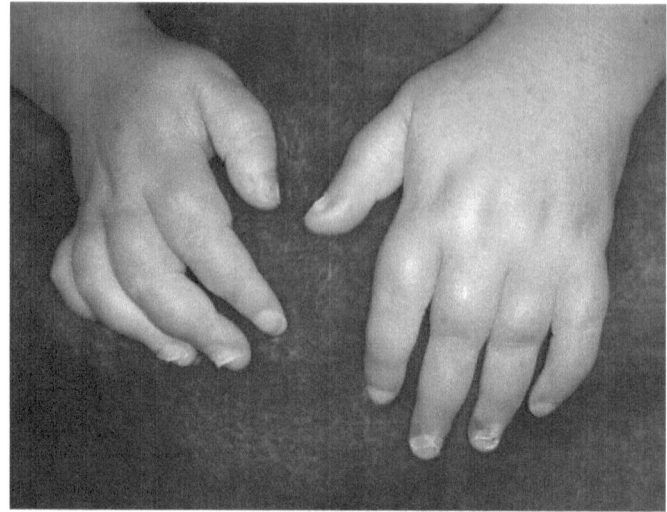

Figure 20. Dactylitis.

Dactylitis is a pathognomonic state of psoriatic arthritis. Another description of the condition is sausage-like fingers. Swelling is of the periarticular rather than the articular.

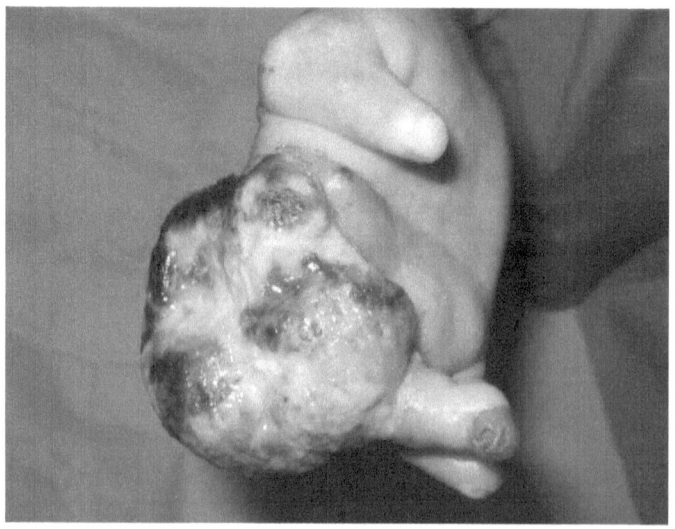

Figure 20. Malignancy in the hand.

The figure above depicts a patient with scleroderma presenting with a non-healing ulcer over her right hand, which turned out to be a squamous cell carcinoma.

Upon inspection, the observer should also look out for the presence of any scar from previous surgery or trauma. The location of the scar suggests possible structures which can be injured. For example, a scar on the medial side of the elbow with presentation of an ulnar claw hand, distally, could most likely be an ulnar nerve palsy that produced the claw hand. A scar over the antecubital fossa, with a pointing index finger, is a highly suggestive sign of high median nerve palsy.

Additionally, hypothenar muscle wasting indicates ulnar nerve palsy, whilst thenar muscle wasting indicates median nerve palsy.

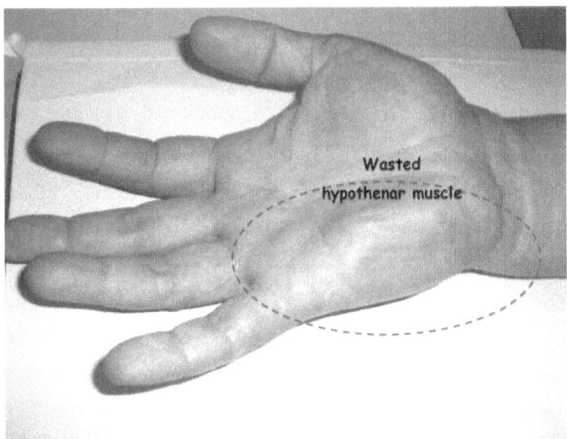

Figure 5. Again with the wasted muscle shown by the dotted circle.

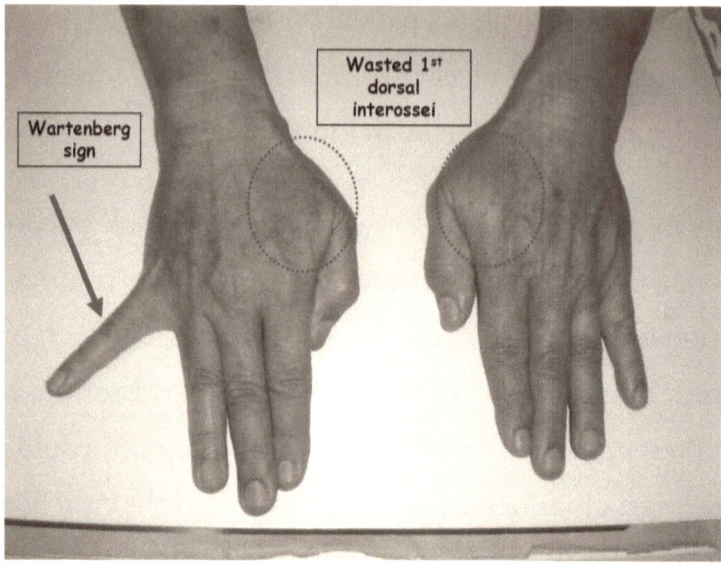

Figure 21. Wartenberg's sign and wasted
muscle in ulnar nerve palsy.

Figure 21 depicts wasted hypothenar and first dorsal interossei muscles in ulnar nerve palsy. Wartenberg's sign is seen due to the weakness of the abductor digiti muscle (ulnar innervated), causing inability to adduct the little finger.

When inspecting swellings of the hands, it is important to differentiate between a benign or malignant swelling.

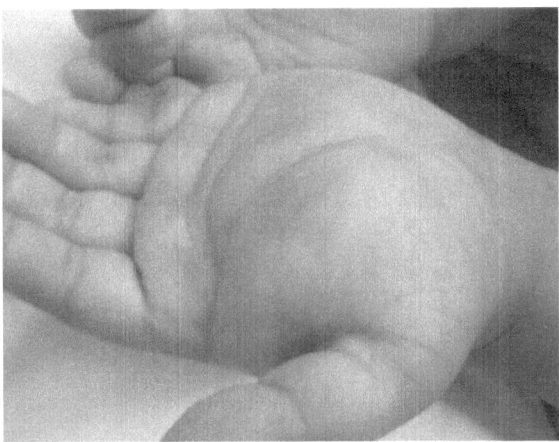

Figure 22. Swelling of the palm.

Figure 22 shows swelling over the palm of a child, which resulted to be a haemangioma.

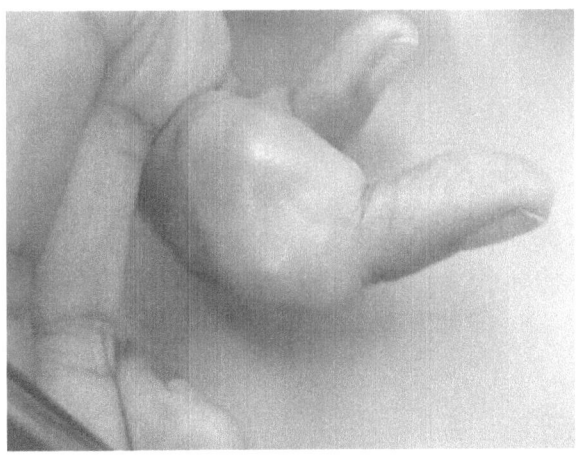

Figure 23. Swelling of the finger.

The above picture shows swelling over the radial palmar of the right ring finger, which resulted to be a giant cell tumour of the tendon sheath. Note the multilobulated appearance of this mass which favour the diagnosis. Giant cell tumour of the tendon sheath is the second most common cause of swelling of the hand. It is benign and differs from giant cell tumours of the bone, which has metastatic potential.

Ganglions

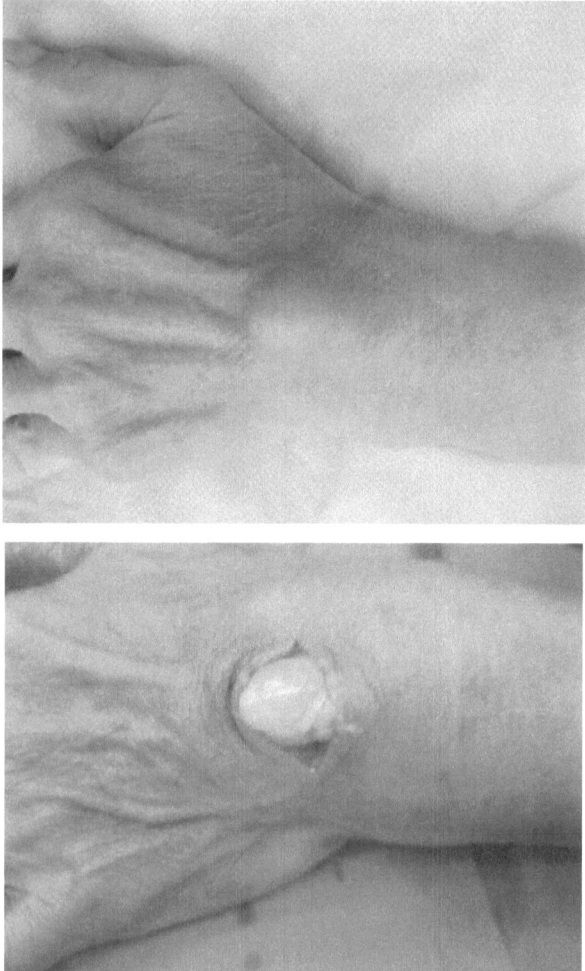

Figure 24. A ganglion.

Figure 24 shows a ganglion, the commonest soft tissue swelling of the hand. Upon excision, the mass contained synovial fluid. It is an outpouching of a weakened portion of a joint capsule or a tendon sheath. Most commonly, it is found over the dorsum of the hand arising from the scapholunate joint. Patients will present with a swelling which fluctuates in size over time.

Trigger Finger

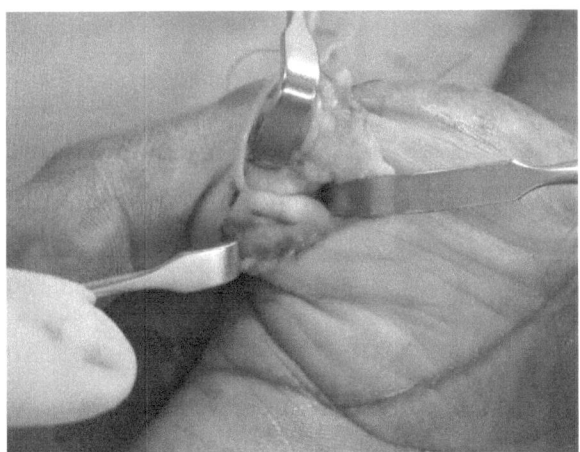

Figure 25. An exposed flexor tendon in trigger finger.

Patients with trigger fingers are commonly mistaken to have osteoarthritis or rheumatoid arthritis as they initially present with vague pain and aches over the metacarpophalangeal areas or the base of the fingers. However, once the patient mentions 'triggering', the diagnosis is easily made and treated. The figure above depicts a swollen and inflamed flexor tendon just proximal to the stenotic A1 pulley, which has been surgically released.

CRPS (Chronic Regional Pain Syndrome)

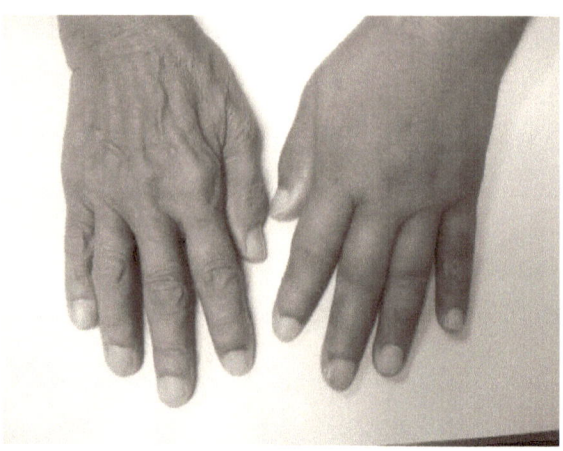

Figure 26. Chronic regional pain syndrome.

Note that the patient's left hand and fingers are swollen in a sausage-like manner, are smooth and hairless, and are also occasionally discoloured. Chronic regional pain syndrome is previously known as reflex sympathetic dystrophy (RSD) and is difficult to treat. Acknowledging the syndrome that exists in the patient is the first step in the treatment.

Glomus Tumour

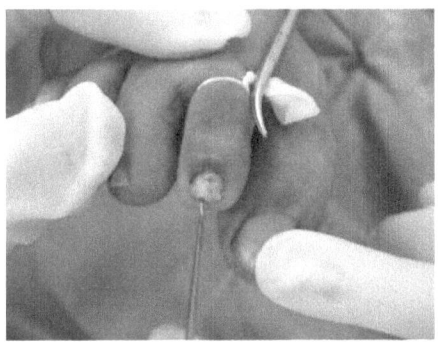

Figure 27. Glomus tumour.

Glomus tumours are rare but an important disease to highlight as patients are typically misdiagnosed for up to ten years. The glomus body is a neuromyoarterial apparatus in the fingertips or toes. Patients are presented with cold intolerance, hypersensitivity to touch, and excruciating pain. Examination reveals a small bluish nodule underneath the nail plate. The picture above was taken after the nail plate had been removed, exposing the pink glomus tumour.

Pyogenic Granuloma

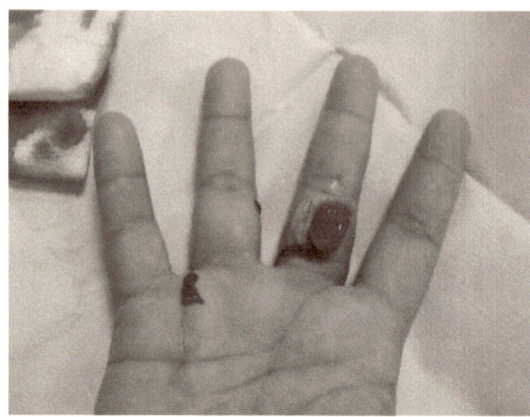

Figure 28. Pyogenic granuloma.

The figure above shows a fungating-like friable mass over the left middle finger. Although it looks alarming, the mass is a pyogenic granuloma—a misnomer—as no infection or granulomas is present. It is easily excised.

Squamous Cell Carcinoma

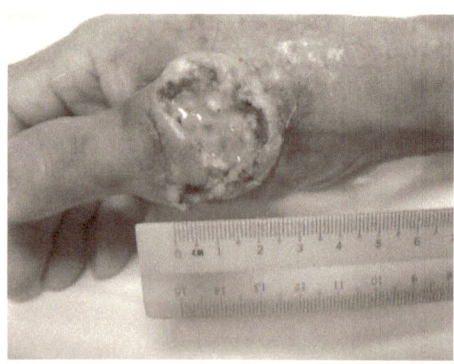

Figure 29. A squamous cell carcinoma.

The above picture shows a squamous cell carcinoma of the base of the thumb.

Chronic Fungal Infection

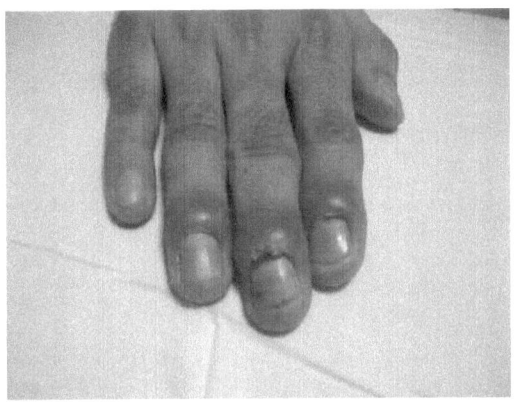

Figure 30. Infected fingers.

The figure above shows three fingers with a chronic fungal infection for a span of two years, with ulcerated and inflamed eponychial areas. Treatment involves surgical excision of the and anti-fungal agents.

10.4. Palpation

Joint warmness should be palpated using the back of the hands as this area has fewer sweat glands. Candidates can also perspire a lot during their exams, thus making the palmar a poor choice. The DIP, PIP, and wrists of both hands should be palpated and compared with the extensor part of the elbow.

Joint tenderness is determined by using two thumbs to press on each side of the joint. The colour of the lower part of the nail bed of the thumbs should be white during this manoeuver. The candidate will have to press all the joints, and at all times, the candidate must observe for pain in the patient's facial expression. Therefore, if the joints are warm, they will be tender.

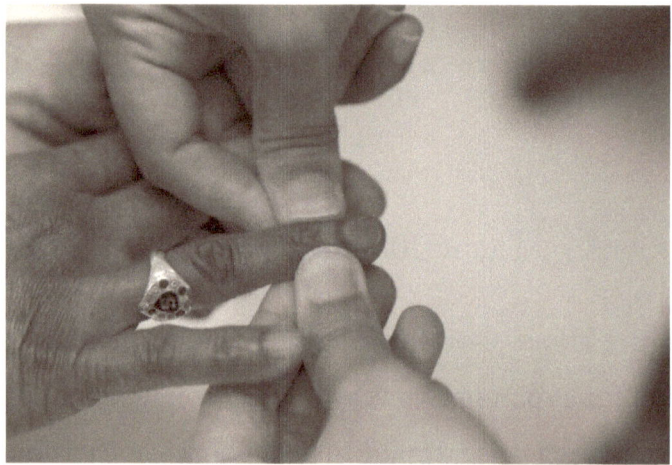

Figure 31. Pressing of the joints with both thumbs.

The overlying skin between the joints should be pinched, especially in sclerodactyly hands. This is to determine the Rodnan score.[69]

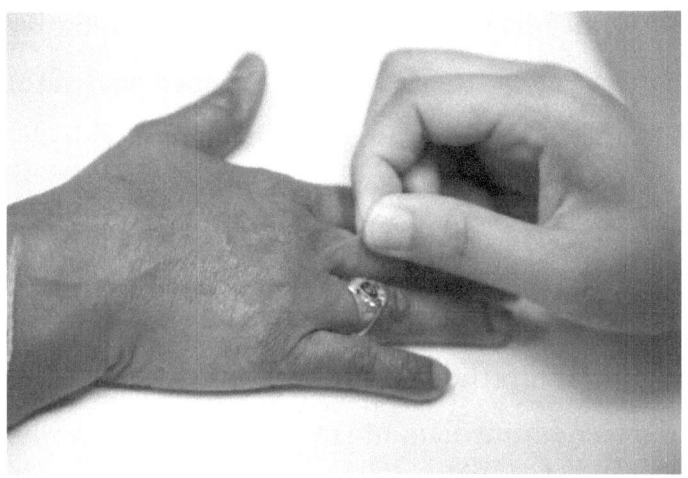

Figure 32. Pinching of the overlying skin.

Also palpate for the identification of tophi.

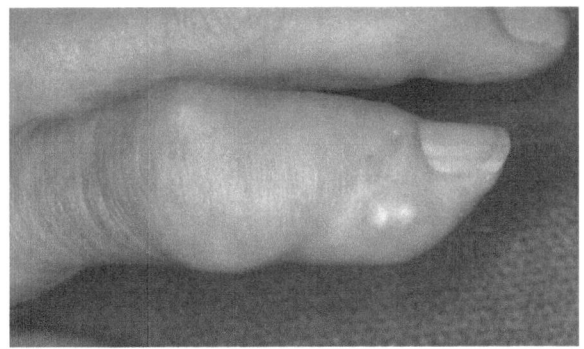

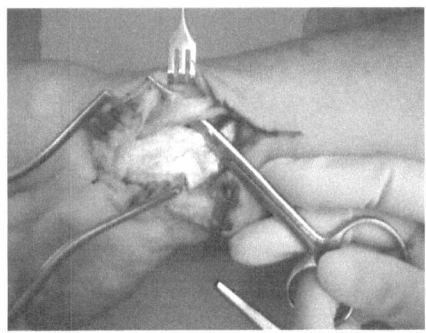

Figure 33. Tophi.

In the bottom image, a gouty tophi had been removed from the volar aspect of a patient's wrist, which had resulted in carpal tunnel compression. Note the chalky whitish colour of the tophi.

10.5. Neurology

For neurology, start the first step with the Kumar.[70] This test is done to screen for median, ulnar, or radial nerve involvement. In rheumatoid arthritis, vasculitis and nerve palsies can occur. The correct performance of this test requires all the fingers to be fanned out with an extended wrist, except for the index finger and the thumb.

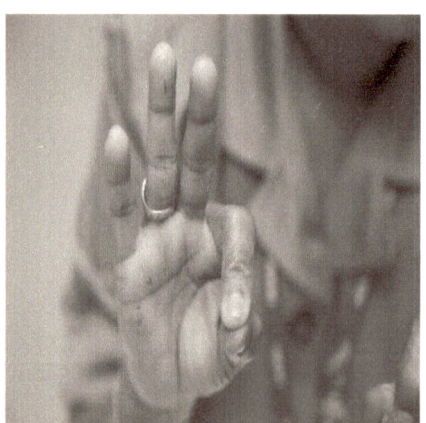 

Figure 34. Patient undergoing the Kumar test.

However, in severely deformed hands, movements are most often restricted, especially at the wrists, but if the patient is able to extend the wrists, a wrist drop may be excluded. If positive, further confirmatory tests should be done for each nerve involvement. Patients with median nerve palsy will not be able to flex the DIPJ of the index finger and IPJ of the thumb due to paralysis of the FDP up to the index finger and the FPL, which are both supplied by the median nerve.

For the ulnar nerve, one has to examine for Froment's sign. Froment's sign is positive in patient with ulnar nerve palsy because of the paralysis of the thumb adductor muscle that is supplied by the ulnar nerve. Patients with ulnar nerve palsy will use the FPL (supplied by the median nerve) to prevent the doctor from pulling the piece of paper, resulting in flexion of the thumb IPJ.

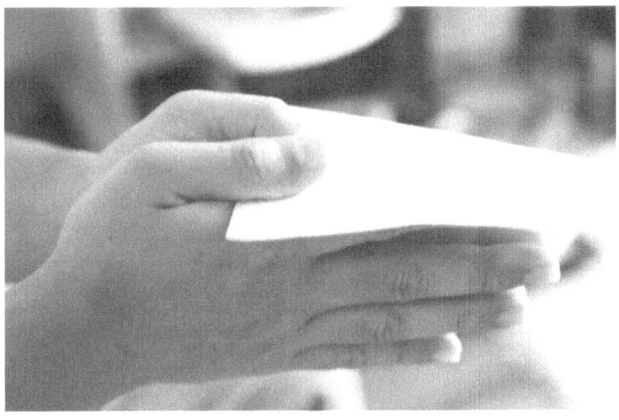

Figure 35. Patient holding a piece of paper with the thumbs in an examination of the Froment's sign.

For the median nerve, the patient is instructed to make an interlock with all the fingers of both hands together or to make a fist. The index finger will not be able to be flexed or be bent, producing a 'pointing index finger sign'. This is seen only in high median nerve palsy due to paralysis of both FDS and FDP of the index finger, which is supplied by the median nerve.

Occasionally, both index and middle fingers are not able to be flexed or bent, and if the middle finger's FDP is totally supplied by only the median nerve and not dually innervated by the median and ulnar nerve, the 'benediction sign' is produced.

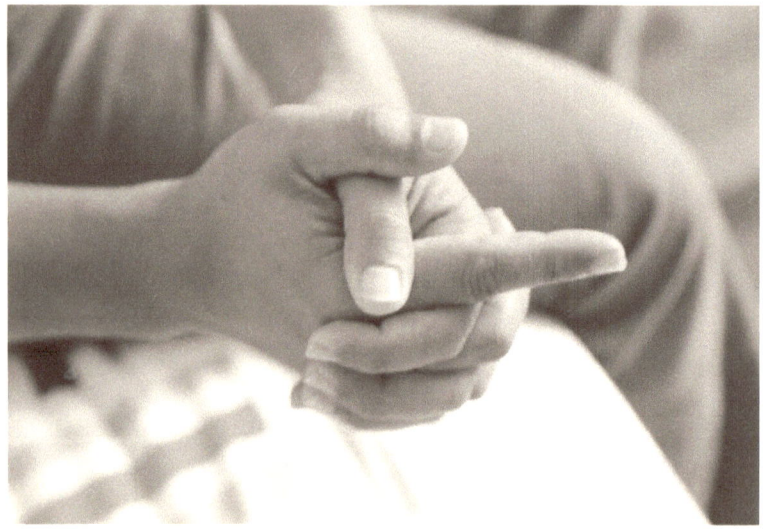

Figure 36.

For the radial nerve, the candidate must examine for dorsiflexion of the wrist and the fingers at the MCP joints for a wrist and finger drop. Wrist drop is due to paralysis of the ECRL muscle, and finger drop is due to paralysis of all the extensor muscles of the forearm.

When examining for finger drop, it is important that the wrist is extended by the candidate so that the finger extension is fully performed by the finger extensors. If the wrist is in a flexed position and the patient is instructed to extend the fingers, the motion would be performed by the lumbricals.

Figure 37.

The next stage is the assessment of muscle strength of the small muscles of the hands, beginning with the interossei muscle abduction and adduction (ulnar nerve innervated).

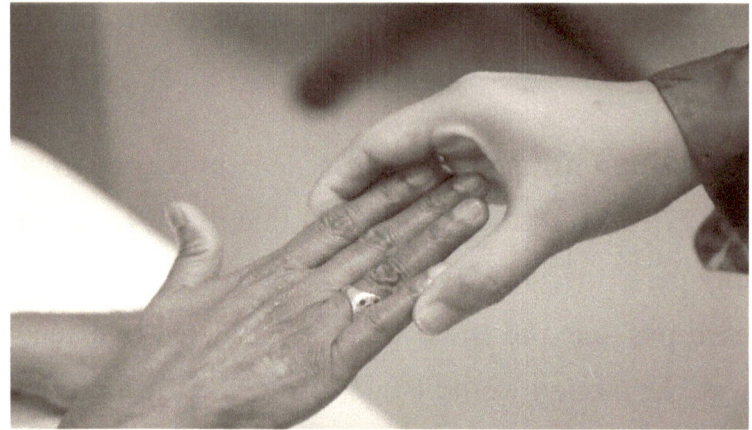

Figure 38.

Testing abductor pollicis brevis muscle
(median nerve innervated).

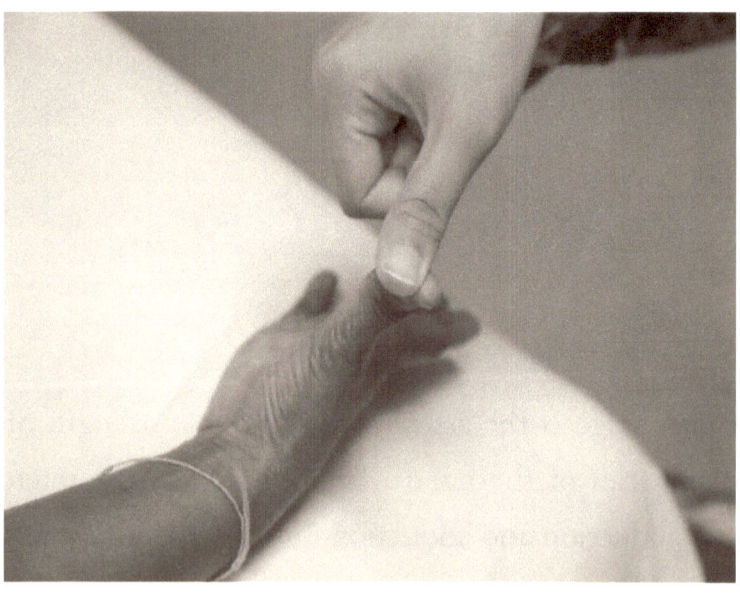

Figure 39.

Testing the opponens pollicis (median nerve innervated).

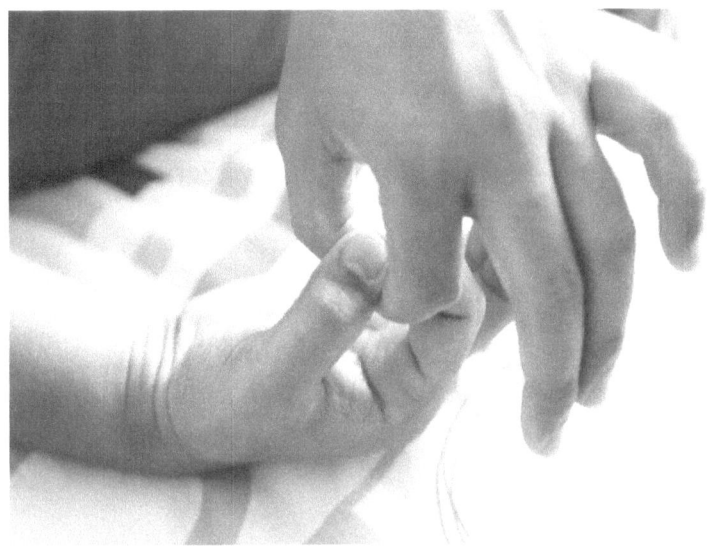

Figure 40.

This is followed by pinprick testing of C6 (tip of thumb), C7 (tip of middle finger), and C8 (tip of little finger). This should be done with the skin of the chest or forehead as the reference point and with the patient's eyes closed.

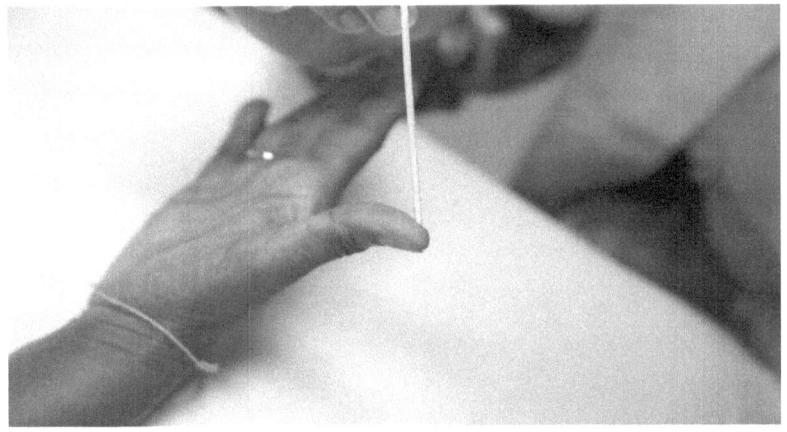

Figure 41.

10.6. Testing the Tendons[71]

Flexors of both the flexor digitorum superficialis and profundus should be tested for tendon integrity.

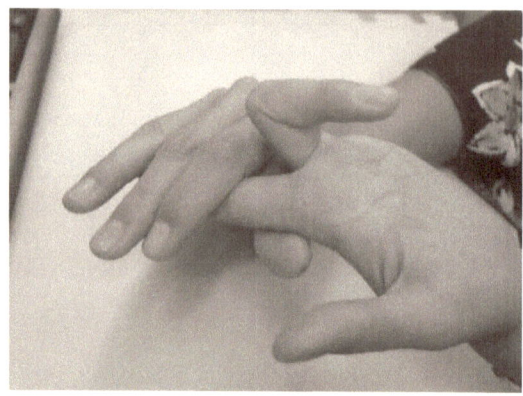

Figure 42. Testing flexor digitorum superficialis.

FDP to the middle, ring, and small fingers shares a common proximal origin. The other fingers need to be resisted when testing the FDS of another finger.

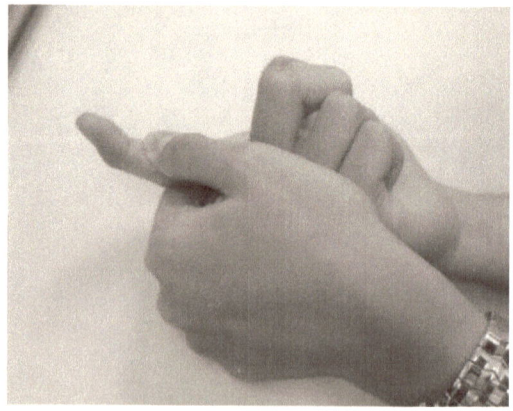

Figure 43. Testing the FDP tendon. The technique is the same for all the fingers.

10.7. Functional Assessment

There are various methods for this test. The patient can be requested to write his/her name, button and unbutton his/her shirt, comb the hair, and lock the door with a key.

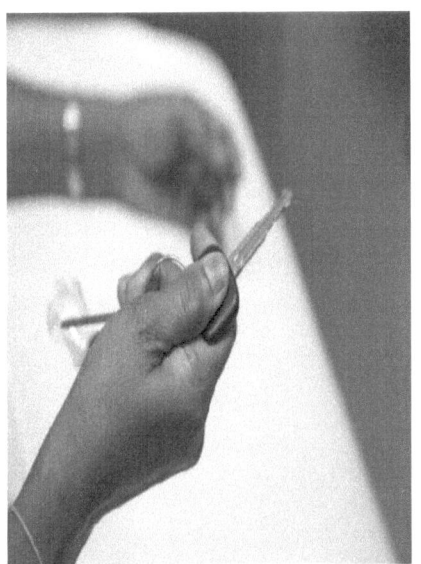 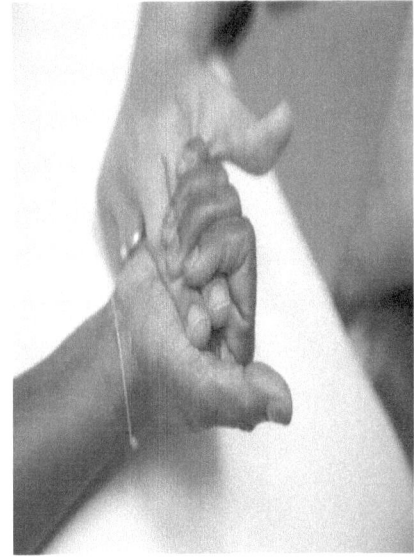

Figure 44. Patient conducting tasks
during functional assessment.

Often after a stylish and smooth performance, time will not be a problem. A candidate should palpate the elbows for subcutaneous nodules and auscultate posteriorly for fine crepitations over the lower lung bases.

11.0

CONCLUSION

By this time, dear reader, you should be standing up straight, eyes brimming with confidence, and hands behind your back, stating the diagnosis as active/remission rheumatoid arthritis with good/poor functional capacity. Do not forget to include one or two differential diagnosis to complete your examination.

12.0

RADIOLOGY

Modalities such as hand radiograph of the anteroposterior and oblique views, musculoskeletal ultrasounds, and magnetic resonance imaging (MRI) exist in radiology.

12.1. Hand Radiographs

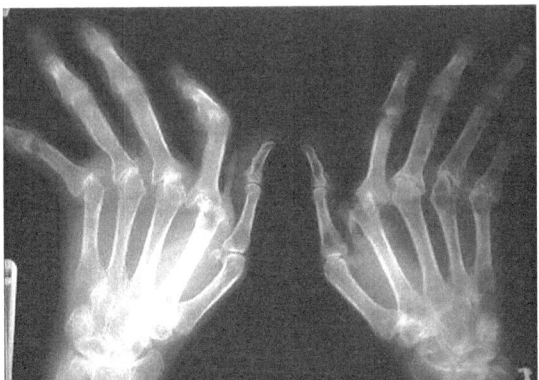

Figure 45. Radiograph of hands with

In Figure 45, subcutaneous swellings can be visualised by the soft tissue shadow swelling around the hands. The second step involves recognising periarticular osteopenia. The third step is very specifically observing for the reduction of the joints. The fourth step is appreciating the periosteal reaction and the erosions. The fifth step is recognising subluxations. The final step is looking for fractures.

12.2. Ultrasound of the Hands and Wrists

In this section, a focus is made on ultrasound (US) pathology of the hands and wrists.

Main abnormalities that will be examined are synovitis, synovial hypertrophy, joint erosions, and tenosynovitis.[72] In US terms, *synovial effusion* means completely transonic, compressible, and with no increase in Doppler signal.[73] On the other hand, *synovial hypertrophy* is defined as non-displaceable, intra-articular, poorly compressible tissue, which may exhibit Doppler signal.[74]

According to McNally, the classification of synovial thickness is recorded using a scale of three levels (1 to 3—mild, moderate, and severe), whereby a moderate synovial thickening is between 2 mm and 4 mm.[75] A three-point scale is also used to record blood flow. Here, *mild* is defined with the presence of only a few scattered vessels in the synovium, *moderate* with less than 50 per cent vascularity, and *severe* with more than 50 per cent vascularity. Finally, 0 and 1 are used to denote the presence or absence of erosions. Colour Doppler flow assessment should therefore accompany all ultrasound examinations of the swollen joint.[76]

MRI of the hands and wrists will not be covered in this book.

13.0

REFERENCES

1   M. Doherty, JD, P. Dieppe, and M. Snaith, 'The "GALS" Locomotor Screen', *Ann Rheum Dis*, 10/51 (1992), 5.

2   Scott R. Grewe, Christopher J. Nanson, Mark B. Wagner, and Brian L. Puskas, *Hand Anatomy* (2020).

3   F. V. Wilder, JPB, and E. J. Farina, 'Joint-Specific Prevalence of Osteoarthritis of the Hand', *Osteoarthritis Cartilage*, 14/9 (2006), 953–7; Teresa Oton and LC, 'The Epidemiology of Established Rheumatoid Arthritis', *Best Pract Res Clin Rheumatol*, 33/5 (2020); C. Peoples, MTJ, M. Lucas, B. L. Rosario, and C. A. Feghali-Bostwick, 'Gender Differences in Systemic Sclerosis: Relationship to Clinical Features, Serologic Status and Outcomes', *J Scleroderma Relat Disord* (2016).

4   Peoples, MTJ, Lucas, Rosario, and Feghali-Bostwick, 'Gender Differences in Systemic Sclerosis'.

5   Wayne Reizner and DAF, 'Boutonniere [Buttonhole] Deformity', Medscape (2019).

6   Ibid.

7   NEA, 'The Rheumatoid Swan-Neck Deformity', *Hand Clin*, 5/2 (1989), 203–14.

8   R. P. Welsh and HD, 'Swan Neck Deformity in Rheumatoid Arthritis of the Hand', *Hand*, 9/2 (1977), 109–16.

9   Michael Neumeister and JAM, 'Hand and Wrist Surgery in Rheumatoid Arthritis', Medscape (2019).

10 Ibid.

11 F. J. van der Giesen, VLW, C. Kremers-Selten, et al., 'Effectiveness of Two Finger Splints for Swan Neck Deformity in Patients with Rheumatoid Arthritis: A Randomized, Crossover Trial', *Arthritis Rheum*, 61/8 (2009), 1025–31.

12 Neumeister and JAM, 'Hand and Wrist Surgery'.

13 BKD, 'The Dorsal Approach to Silicone Implant Arthroplasty of the Proximal Interphalangeal Joint', *J. Hand Surg Am*, 32/6 (2007), 909–13.

14 Neumeister and JAM, 'Hand and Wrist Surgery'.

15 Ibid.

16 A. B. Stein and ALT, 'The Rheumatoid Thumb', *Hand Clin*, 12/3 (1996), 541–550.

17 Ibid.

18 Neumeister and JAM, 'Hand and Wrist Surgery'.

19 Ibid.

20 Ibid.

21 E. A. Nalebuff, FP, and L. H. Millender, 'Rheumatoid Arthritis in the Hand and Wrist', *Green's Operative Hand Surgery* (2nd ed., Churchill Livingstone, 1988).

22 Neumeister and JAM, 'Hand and Wrist Surgery'.

23 Ibid.

24 Ibid.

25 Ibid.

26 Ibid.

27 Ibid.

28 Ibid.

29 J. H. Hsueh, LW, K. C. Yang, K. C. Hsu, C. T. Lin, and L. W. Chen, 'Spontaneous Extensor Tendon Rupture in the Rheumatoid Wrist: Risk Factors and Preventive Role of Extended Tenosynovectomy', *Ann Plast Surg*, 76 (2016).

30 Neumeister and JAM, 'Hand and Wrist Surgery'.

31 Ibid.

32 Ibid.

33 J. S. Smolen, LR, J. W. J. Bijlsma, et al., 'EULAR Recommendations for the Management of Rheumatoid Arthritis with Synthetic and Biological Disease-Modifying Antirheumatic Drugs: 2019 Update', *Ann Rheum Dis*, 73/3 (2020), 492–509.

34 J. L. Barnas and RC, 'Etiology and Pathogenesis of Psoriatic Arthritis', *Rheum Dis Clin North Am*, 41 (2015), 643.

35 FDT, 'An Update on the Pathogenesis and Epidemiology of Osteoarthritis', *Radiol Clin North Am*, 42 (2004), 1–9.

36 ARD, 'Classification of Disease: Osteoarthritis', *Semin Arthritis Rheum*, 20 (1991), 40–47.

37 G. Raimbeau, FP, B. Cesari, M. Le Bourg, and Y. Saint-Cast, 'Arthropathie goutteuse du poignet a propos de cinq cas', *Chirurgie de la Main*, 20 (2001), 325–31.

38 T. Ohishi, KY, M. Takahashi, R. Miyata, and K. Kushida, 'Scapholunate Dissociation Caused by Gouty Arthritis of the

Wrist', *Scand J Plast Reconstr Surg Hand Surg*, 34 (2000), 189–191.

39 Ariel A.Williams, HMC, and Scott D. Lifchez, 'The Scleroderma Hand: Manifestations of Disease and Approach to Management', *The Journal of Hand Surgery*, 43/6 (2018), 550–557.

40 Ibid.

41 R. E. G. S. F. Habusta, 'Ganglion Cyst', StatPearls (StatPearls Publishing, 2021).

42 T. Safran, HJ, B. Al-Halabi, H. Al-Naeem, and S. Cugno, 'Scaphoid Cysts: Literature Review of Etiology, Treatment, and Prognosis', *Hand*, 14/6 (2019), 751–759.

43 J. Meyerson, PY, M. Spaeth, and G. Pearson, 'Pediatric Ganglion Cysts: A Retrospective Review', *Hand PMC*, 14/4 (2019), 445–448.

44 Habusta, 'Ganglion Cyst'.

45 N. L. Ashworth, 'Carpal Tunnel Syndrome', Medscape (2020).

46 RLR, 'Electrodiagnosis of Carpal Tunnel Syndrome', *Phys Med Rehabil Clin N Am*, 18/4 (2017), 733–46; D. Lee, VHM, P. K. Janevski, et al., 'Ultrasound versus Electromyography', *Radiol Clin North Am*, 37/4 (1999).

47 D. O'Connor, MS, and N. Massy-Westropp, 'Non-Surgical Treatment [Other Than Steroid Injection] for Carpal Tunnel Syndrome', Cochrane Database Syst Rev (2003).

48 BCA, 'A Prospective, Nonrandomized Study of Iontophoresis, Wrist Splinting and Antiinflammatory Medication in the Treatment of Early-Mild Carpal Tunnel Syndrome', *J Occup Med*, 36/2 (1994), 166–8.

49 S. Marshall, TG, and N. Ashworth, 'Local Corticosteroid Injection for Carpal Tunnel Syndrome', Cochrane Database Syst Rev (2007).

50 R. J. Scholten, MVDMA, B. M. Uitdehaag, et al., 'Surgical Treatment Options for Carpal Tunnel Syndrome', Cochrane Database Syst Rev (2007).

51 Eva Kovacs and HSD, 'Dupuytren Contracture', Medscape (2020).

52 L. C. Hurst, BM, V. R. Hentz, et al., 'Injectable Collagenase Clostridium Histolyticum for Dupuytren's Contracture', *N Eng J Med*, 361/10 (2009), 968–79.

53 LAR, 'Dupuyteren's Contracture', *Workplace Health Saf*, 65/3 (2017), 96–99.

54 W. Clifford, ed., 'Dupuyteren's Contracture:Orho Preferred', *Wheeless' Textbook of Orthopedics* (2013).

55 S. G. Anthony, LCS, B. P. Simmons, and J. B. Jupiter, 'Gender Ratio of Dupuytren's Disease in the Modern U.S. Population', *Hand*, 3/2 (NY, 2008.), 87–90; AQMM, 'Factors in the Pathogenesis of Dupuytren's Contracture', *J Hand Surg Am*, 31/9 (2006), 1527–34.

56 S. Hindocha, MD, and A. Bayat, 'Epidemiological Evaluation of Dupuytren's Disease Incidence and Prevalence Rates in Relation to Etiology', *Hand*, 4/3 (NY, 2009), 256–69.

57 K. E. Meathrel and TA, 'Abductor Digiti Minimi Involvement in Dupuytren's Contracture of the Small Finger', *J Hand Surg Am*, 29/3 (2004), 510–3.

58 Kovacs and HSD, 'Dupuytren Contracture'.

59 Ibid.

60 Ibid.

61 Ibid.

62 Bradon J. Wilhelm, Leonard J. Weiner, Ian C. Marrero, and Bünyamin Sahin, 'Hand Anatomy, Medscape (2011).

63 Ibid.

64 Ibid.

65 Ibid.

66 Ibid.

67 Ibid.

68 Ibid.

69 Ibid.

70 Louis Solomon, DJW, and Selvadurai Nayagam, *Apley's System of Orthopaedics and Fractures* (2010).

71 Ibid.

72 E. G. McNally, 'Ultrasound of the Small Joints of Hands and Feet: Current Status', *Skeletal* Radiol, 37 (2008), 99–113.

73 Ibid.

74 Ibid.

75 Ibid.

76 Ibid.

www.ingramcontent.com/pod-product-compliance
Lightning Source LLC
Chambersburg PA
CBHW050419290526
45786CB00003B/1326